Rhansym Crosses The Rainbow Bridge

Suzy Buckles

ISBN: 978-1-54394-949-0

This book is dedicated to all of the loving members of my pet loss group on Facebook. The group is titled PET LOSS & HEALING SUPPORT TO THE TRAIN OF RECOVERY.

ACKNOWLEDGEMENTS

A special thank you to Marni Zats Alvino, my co-administrator. Thank you also to Carol Goldman Siegel, Toni Cielo, and Lisa Smelser Shifflett, who are also administrators of this very special group.

A great thank you to my artist friend, Karen Duffy McPherson, for allowing me to use her gorgeous painting for a background picture on page 39 of my book.

Thanks to two of my grandchildren, Allie & Jake Eikenberry, whose artwork is on pages 11 and 16. Also, another talented grandson, Zach Cianciolo, did two pieces of art, hanging on a wall on page 3. Thank you to the three of you!

Wendy and her two children, Allie and Jake, lived in Navarre, Florida. It was a lovely, happy place for them, until their pet, Rhansym, passed. Dr. Spears, their veterinarian, had to euthanize the dog due to his dire physical condition.

The pets at the Rainbow Bridge were thrilled to welcome another patient of Dr. Spears. Dr. Spears was their hero!

Everyone at the Rainbow Bridge was getting ready to
greet Rhansym. Alfie and Bertie directed the celebration.
Rhansym could arrive at any moment!

The pets overheard some people back on Earth who were thinking that perhaps Dr. Spears had ended Rhansym's life too soon.

"Maybe Rhansym could have lived longer,"
Wendy lamented. Wendy and her friends began
to protest outside of Dr. Spears' office.

Dr. Spears and his colleagues felt quite troubled
by this. He cared so deeply for all of his patients.
Whenever someone had lost a beloved pet, he always
encouraged them to hop on the Train of Recovery,
a loving pet loss group to help with the pain.

But life at the Rainbow Bridge carried on with much happiness.

Still, the pets were concerned for Dr. Spears, as they knew that he was a God-send to them.

**"Those folks should hop onto the Train of Recovery,"
said Annie to Cooper, Chelsea, and Rosie.**

All of the pets agreed. Pet Loss & Healing Support to the Train of Recovery was a wondrous helper to those who had lost their pets. It was a soothing, comforting group where others who had gone through the same thing were there to do nothing but help those who were hurting from loss.

"We all want you to be happy as we are here!" said beloved Trixy.

"Our hearts all remain with you
who are on Earth.
Please believe this truth!"

Meanwhile, people at the vet's office overheard the issues outside; people protesting their beloved Dr. Spears.

The pets had decided that this
was too much, that they had
to do something to clear
Dr. Spears' name on Earth.

The pets were still awaiting the arrival of Rhansym.
Angel Babette and her beloved Shelby
watched for him, to no avail.

They all knew that Rhansym's owners were struggling
with massive grief and that they suspected perhaps
Dr. Spears had been at fault for his early demise.

Everyone continued to welcome newcomers to the Rainbow Bridge. It was a fabulous new world where all pets would one day be reunited with their owners!

Dash and Don gathered some pets together
and began to sing songs - comforting music.
They knew that Rhansym would show up soon,
especially once everyone's heart was put to rest,
knowing that Rhansym's time had come on Earth.

The singing continued and the pets knew in their hearts that the anguish felt on Earth would diminish shortly.

Quila grew tired from all of the singing.
It was time for bed.

The next morning, the pets began to think about how
they could show everyone on Earth, particularly in Navarre,
that Dr. Spears was an awesome veterinarian and that he had
protected Rhansym from further suffering, sending him to
his permanent home at the Rainbow Bridge.

The pets gathered in groups, chatting about how to show people on Earth that Dr. Spears was a true wonder!

I had to say goodbye to my sweet little babie emmie
you know she was very ill it was the hardest thing I've ever

Sassie

Mr. Kitty

Baghira

OSCAR   Melanie   PANCHO

Sutch

Alfie & Bertie

Ashley

Ashley   Ash

Ashley

Coope

CHICO

Sweetie

Shelby   Presley   CLEO   Charlie

Emmie

Bubbles

Ron

They decided to gather balloons, kites, and flowers to shower on Dr. Spears' lawn.

That would be an amazing sight for the people there in Navarre to see!

**The next day, the angels and pets went
shopping for delights with which
to fashion Dr. Spears' yard, an adornment
to show Dr. Spears' real character!**

Precious, Anakin, and Rocky said prayers for Dr. Spears, as well as for Wendy, Allie, and Jake, Rhansym's Earthly family.

**Kitties played hide-and-seek while Scoop, Andy,
and Greta reflected on their beloved parents on Earth.**

Then, all of the pets joined in, playing
and sending their love to their Earthly parents.

8-Ball and Axl were sad, as they missed their mommies so much. Chico, Scarlett, and Maddie comforted them, letting them know that they could view them from their dimension. All that was important was that the owners be on the mend!

**Happiness and joy lifted their spirits, however,
as they knew things would soon work out for the people
on Earth. They just wanted their Earthly parents
to understand that they're still with them!**

The pets prayed that those who continued in pain would get onto the Train of Recovery.

All of the pets continued to pray.

They knew that the prayers would work.

With this knowledge, celebrations began!

All of the angels and pets
knew that the anguish would
soon be over.

Loving community members held a get-together for Dr. Spears. They let him know that if it wasn't for him, their pets wouldn't have had such wonderful, pain-free lives!

At that same moment, Rhansym appeared at
the Rainbow Bridge. Everyone there was totally
delighted! Their prayers had been answered!
Things were settling down on Earth!

**Rhansym and a beautiful girl named Lizzie had just been married,
as well as other amazing couples. It was a super day!**

The next morning, the miracle happened. The yard of Dr. Spears' office was embellished with magical pets, flowers, balloons, kites, and excitement!

Celebrations began to kick up in Navarre. A huge crowd swarmed J.J. Chago's restaurant, where music, dancing, and dining were greatly enjoyed. Everyone was excited. The people KNEW that Dr. Spears was their true hero! Wendy, Allie, and Jake were overwhelmed with relief and happiness!

Rhansym

Lizzie

Train of Recovery